C L Y D E

Rock Villa

Seafield Cottage

Villa Marita

Clyde Bank

Bagatelle

Glenpark

Bellevue

B.M.10.5

Seafield

Seabank

Quarrybank

B.M.13.1

Seafield House

... Cottage

Hillhead

Springbank

107

109

Springfield

110

Beltrees

MARGARET STREET

FORSYTH

LOW COCKROAD

B.M.80.9

BAY OF QUICK

Images of
Greenock

Images of
GREENOCK

Anthony J J McNeill

Argyll
publishing

First published 1998
Argyll Publishing
Glendaruel
Argyll PA22 3AE

**British Library Cataloguing-in-
Publication Data.
A catalogue record for this book is
available from the British Library.**

ISBN 1 874640 04 1 paperback
ISBN 1 874640 09 2 hardback

Origination
Cordfall Ltd, Glasgow

Printing
St Edmundsbury Press

Generous support for this book was available from many sources throughout its compilation. The excellent photograph of John B Scrymgeour was supplied by Burniston Studios Ltd. Inverclyde Council's Watt Library kindly granted use of the photographs on Town Centre Slum Tenement Housing and Smillie & Robson, Fruit and Vegetable Merchants. Much appreciation is also due to George J Freer, Robert Grieves and John Curdy for providing several other views. Access to Lloyd's Yacht Register and yachting journals was granted by Ian P C MacKenzie and the staff at the Royal Gourock Yacht Club. Glasgow City Archives supplied assistance with the Ardgowan Estate Papers. In addition, considerable encouragement was given by Lesley Couperwhite, Tom Johnstone, Neil Paton, May Kohn, David N Allan, Christine Robb, Johnston F Robb and James Hunter. Numerous other people and organisations throughout Scotland contributed the small but essential pieces of information which are so often necessary to complete an enterprise like this one.

Anthony J J McNeill
Gourock April 1998

Introduction

Local photographs always attract much curiosity. The selection in this book is the work of various townspeople who had the great foresight to record many aspects of Greenock in pictures over the years. Sadly, none of the very early photographers are known today. It is possible, however, to name a few of their successors. John Boden Scrymgeour, a notable local character, accumulated a particularly fine wide-ranging collection of glass lantern slides and prints between the 1870s and the 1950s. Similar high quality material during this period was produced by G W Wilson, a plumber in the town. George Freer, butler to Robert L Scott, Chairman of Scott's Shipbuilding & Engineering Company Limited, took advantage of his position to obtain superb interior views of Balclutha, his employer's West End mansion, in the 1930s. More recent photographers include D H B McNeill, my father, who collected maritime views as well as town scenes.

J B Scrymgeour is a most significant member of this group of people. Contemporaries always thought of him as a slim, fairly tall person with iron grey hair, a beard, bright eyes and quick precise speech. Everyone regarded him as a fine man – even though most acquaintances dreaded trying to keep up with his spry walking pace in the street. Honest, teetotal, kind, stern with fair but strong views, he treated other people as equals and his conversation was said to have included always "matters worthy of consideration".

John was born in 1877. Elizabeth and Archibald Scrymgeour, his parents, came to Greenock from Ballymena in Northern Ireland around 1870. They had a family of thirteen children but as was common at the time, only John and three others survived to adulthood. Archibald was a linen weaver employed locally as a sugarhouse worker.

From an early age, John Scrymgeour was fascinated with local history and photography. These passions were enthusiastically pursued throughout his life. Often a friend would act as his plate camera and equipment caddie on trips around the town. Many pictures illustrated news stories in the *Greenock Telegraph* and books about the town's history. Some even adorned the letterhead paper of local organisations such as the Old Quay Head Trades' Amateur Rowing Club.

By 1900, John was a master grocer and provisions merchant with his own shop at 53 Main Street, on the Cartsburn Street corner, supplying Eastenders and the ships in local docks. Local newsworthy picture postcards made from his photographs were displayed alongside the grocery merchandise. Around 1909, he transferred the business to 21 Rue End Street, just a little west of Arthur Street at Charing Cross, which became familiar premises to many people.

J B Scrymgeour acquired his own flat on the upper floor of Dunedin, a large house on St Lawrence Street. It had a marvellous view westwards over the town towards Helensburgh and the Gareloch. Living in bachelorhood, he kept the place in a state of total clutter but he always knew the exact location of everything. Visitors were welcome. A friend arriving at his home on a winter evening would see that the parlour curtains were drawn together but a chink of gas mantle light had been left at the top. This was a sign indicating that he was ready to receive his guest. Once the person was inside, John would quickly draw the curtains properly together. Inevitably, a vigorous discussion about Greenock's past would follow. When supper came along, it often included examples of his cooking like rhubarb pudding or rich fruit dumpling. Another debate would ensue afterwards. When it was late, John would put on an overcoat, turn the gas mantles down low and accompany his companion part of the way homewards.

Even with a thriving grocery business, John Scrymgeour found time during the 1910s and 1920s to serve as a councillor and latterly as a bailie in the Corporation of Greenock. He was one of several people who represented Cartsdyke district's population. It is quite clear that serving on the Housing, Streets, Cleansing, Gas and Water Committees were his principal concerns. However, John was also a member of the Concerts Committee, at one point helping to arrange a recital of George Erideric Handel's music in the Town Hall, Municipal Buildings.

John, of course, led a full life in other ways. He took an active role in the Greenock Ramblers' Club by guiding members to places of

John Boden Scrymgeour (1877–1963)

historical interest around the district. He was also a member of
Greenock Camera Club for many years. When it became known in
1929 that the tenement birthplace of William Quarrier, founder of
Quarrier's Homes near Bridge of Weir, on Cross Shore Street was to be
demolished, he suggested that the archway entrance to the building
should be preserved in some way as it was the centenary of the
founder's birth. John's proposal resulted in the arch being rebuilt as
the Quarrier's Homes War Memorial.

John Scrymgeour retired from working life at the grocery shop around
1937. With time to fill, he gave illustrated local history lectures with
titles such as *Reminiscences of Old Greenock, Gleanings from Ancient*

Records of the Old West Kirk, Greenock or *Historical Landmarks of Old Greenock* at Band of Hope religious temperance movement gatherings, church functions and club meetings using a large brass and wood projector to show about 80 of his glass slides. These talks were often held twice a day with around 200 people in the audiences.

Typically, he came out of retirement to serve the community throughout the Second World War. As the Assistant Manager in the Greenock East End Co-operative Society's shop on East Crawford Street, he naturally attracted many of his old customers into the premises. Groceries were on display at one side of the store, cakes and teabread were available at the other side of the shop.

After the war, J B Scrymgeour continued his local studies talks for many years including a session with St Margaret's Church Men's Guild in the 1950s, when demand from the womenfolk was so great that they were allowed to attend the meeting as well. Around this time, he also took up family history research for other people. One project which gave him much pleasure was a special investigation into William Marshall & Son, tanners, skinners and wool merchants at the Ladyburn Tanworks many years earlier, for the Marshall family who had emigrated to New Zealand.

My father told me he met him in Cathcart Square just before he died in 1963, aged 86 years. They had a robust conversation, as usual, about everyday and historical matters. Then, John Scrymgeour's quickly retreating figure, brandishing his favourite walking stick, disappeared along the street into the East End of the town. It was a most fitting occasion for a last encounter. My father inherited his fine collection of local history photographs. Now, I have become their custodian.

John Boden Scrymgeour, G W Wilson, George Freer, D H B McNeill and the others have provided us with a splendid insight into earlier times in Greenock. People, shops, churches, streets, harbours, transport, mansions, shipbuilding, factories, parades, sugar refining, parks, disasters and quarrying all feature in their work. They enjoyed sharing these pictures with other people. This book continues that tradition.

a skyline view of the Inchgreen
Gasworks

Glebe and Inchgreen Gasworks

Greenock Corporation built the Glebe Gasworks in 1827–1828 on the
southwestern corner of Laird Street and Crawford (Crawfurd) Street,
now a part of Dalrymple Street at this spot. Its coal gas was mainly
used to provide street lighting. People found the brilliant illumination a
great novelty as everybody was accustomed to oil lamps. A few local
businesses such as the Verreville Glass Warehouse were also early gas
users. During 1828–1829, 516 tons of coal provided some 3 million
cubic feet of energy to 522 customers. Over the years regular
improvements and an occasional extension to the premises coped with
increasing demand from the community. By 1869, though, it was
unable to accommodate any further expansion of its facilities.
Accordingly, the Inchgreen Gasworks was constructed as a
replacement in 1871–1873 along the shore near Port Glasgow. Railway
sidings were located beside the installation to allow convenient delivery
of coal supplies.

an early view of Glebe Gasworks

During the 1921 Coal Strike, almost 7,000 tons of coal were imported
from the United States of America at the James Watt Dock to prevent
the gasworks and other associated facilities closing down. Similar
circumstances arose with the General Strike in 1926. By then, an
entire range of gas appliances like clothes washboilers, cookers,
tenement stairlights, bakery ovens and engineering furnaces had come
into use. Nationalisation took place in 1949 and was followed by
substantial renovation of equipment at the plant to fulfil modern
requirements. Later on, the works formed a part of the West of
Scotland gas supply network. In 1958–1959, 81,230 tons of coal
yielded almost 2 billion cubic feet of energy for 30,950 consumers. The
British Gas Corporation closed these premises in 1964 when cheaper
gas produced by oilfired installations and the availability of the
national grid to distribute it made the place redundant. Its demolition
followed shortly afterwards.

Firth of Clyde Dry Dock

All round the world in the 1950s, shipyards were constructing larger
and larger vessels. The requirement for a giant dry dock on Clydeside
to maintain these ships inevitably became a matter of the highest
priority. During 1960, therefore, the Firth of Clyde Dry Dock Company
Limited was formed by a group of prominent shipbuilding, marine
engineering and associated companies to build and operate a dock
with comprehensive ancillary facilities. Inchgreen was chosen as its
site despite some local preference for a position at the Battery Park.
Development work on this project, capable of handling ships up to
150,000 tons, began in 1961. The photographs show the complex
roughly midway to completion a couple of years later. The 1,000 feet
long by 145 feet wide and 50 feet deep dock with its repair quay, oil
tanker cleaning and gas-freeing installation, high load capacity
electric travelling cranes, workshops, offices and general service
equipment was finished in 1964. *Devonia*, one of the British India
Steam Navigation Company Limited's 12,795-ton school ships, had
the honour of being the first vessel to enter the dry dock. This
venerable cruise liner needed urgent repairs after being in a collision
with an ore carrier at Princes Pier. Some damage can just be seen in
the picture. Near the end of that year, the new works were formally
opened by Princess Mary, the Princess Royal. *British Admiral*, the first
100,000-ton oil tanker completed in the United Kingdom, then arrived
for essential maintenance work prior to sea trials and acceptance by
the BP Tanker Company Limited. This contract was a significant coup
as it supplied tangible evidence that the dry dock could handle very
large vessels. Afterwards, the Cunard Steam Ship Company Limited's
Queen Elizabeth, 83,673 tons, berthed for a multi-million pound refit
so that the liner could exploit the newly burgeoning cruise market.
Around 1970, Scott Lithgow Limited, the Greenock and Port Glasgow
shipbuilders, took over control of the business, giving it their own
name. Under this new ownership, major repairs were carried out to
Ocean Bridge, a 100,000-ton ore/bulk/oil carrier owned by Bibby
Brothers & Company Limited which had suffered a disastrous
explosion and fire at sea while operating with the Seabridge bulk
shipping partnership. *World Scholar*, a tanker of 267,390 tons built by
the company for Niarchos (London) Limited in separate bow and stern

Devonia, in 1964, was the first vessel to use the dry dock

sections was joined afloat at the repair quay, using a submerged cofferdam for the underwater welding process, shortly thereafter. This was an unusual technique carried out with several other massive oil tankers at the quayside. *Atlantic Conveyor*, a 25,000-ton roll-on/roll-off container vessel also owned by the Cunard Steam Ship Company Limited but trading with the Atlantic Container Lines consortium docked later for a lengthening project which increased the size of the cargo freighter to 58,000 tons. Successful completion of the work took place well inside the time limit set by the contract. Trading problems encumbering Scott Lithgow Limited, however, brought about its closure in 1988. Although the Clyde Port Authority, now restructured as Clydeport PLC, was quick to purchase the complex, its future seemed very bleak. The dry dock lay unused for years. But, during 1996, UIE Scotland Limited took a long lease of the premises for marine construction work in the offshore oil industry. Subsequently, Esso Norge AS's *Balder*, a 53,472-ton floating production, storage and offloading unit, arrived for major engineering work and extensive modification of technical equipment on board the vessel. Prospects appear good again.

the flint mill on the Cartsburn near Auchmountain Glen.

Flint Mill

During 1823, the Clyde Pottery Company built a flint mill on Kilmacolm Road, alongside the Cartsburn near Auchmountain Glen, to grind flint for its pottery in Greenock. The millhouse, stable and water trough bringing supplies from the mill dam were wooden, only the kiln and wheelhouse were constructed of stone. Flints were heated to 1,000°C in the kiln to make them brittle then pulverised in water between two millstones. The resulting watery mixture was dried over brick stoves and dispatched to the pottery in barrels where it was blended with other clays making a creamware body used in the production of earthenware goods.

Misfortune struck at 11 o'clock on the night of Saturday, 21 November, 1835 when the Whinhill Reservoir or Beath's Dam which restrained the main source of the Cartsburn burst its eastern embankment after three days of particularly high rainfall. In the millhouse, Archibald Davie, the miller, heard the thunderous noise of its collapse and dashed outside with his family to safety. A torrent of water rushed down on the mill, flattening the house, smashing the waterwheel's wooden trough, demolishing a 3-feet thick wheelhouse wall, covering the wheel with debris to a height of eight feet, sweeping away the millhorse together with its stable and washing fifty tons of flints down the waterway. Nearby, the road was destroyed in places and stout bridges were carried away. Downhill in the town, 38 lives were lost and extensive damage was done to property throughout Cartsdyke. Public concern over this disaster resulted in the establishment of a relief fund to aid people in distressed circumstances.

The flint mill was quickly rebuilt with stone materials, except for another wooden trough, remaining in operation up to the 1850s. Subsequently, a woollen finisher took over the premises for some ten years, after which the property was unoccupied for a long time, probably falling into ruinous condition. Later, however, it became the Auchmountain Steam Laundry until around 1906. Demolition followed in due course.

East Crawford Street

Octavia Cottages comprising English style semidetached brick dwellings, situated beside the near foreground of this 1925 picture, were specially built in 1866–1867 by a working class housing society for artisan families. Plans to erect more homes failed because artisans often could not afford the cost of these premises and few seemingly understood the advantages of cottage life such as a garden and a clothes drying green over their existing squalid living conditions in the town centre.

Opposite these cottages, Craigieknowes Farm occupied land originally held by Mains Farm. Farming came to an end with the progress of urban development in this area during the 1930s. Hillend Public School, a neighbourhood primary school for 900 children including 225 infants, further along the same side of the road, came into service during 1886.

On a new Hillend School being constructed at the Mains Farm site in 1973–1974, the original premises were razed to the ground under redevelopment plans. Its change of name to Oakfield Primary School took place in 1993.

Beyond the school, the distinctive tenement on the far corner of Craigieknowes Street was familiarly known to everybody as the 'Tartan Land' from its red, cream and grey chequered stonework. Hillend House, at the western end of the road, was opened by the Greenock & District Mission to the Deaf & Dumb in 1950 to provide church, lecture hall, kitchen, reading room, ladies' lounge, games room, photographic dark room and workshop facilities for these people. The Glasgow & West of Scotland Society for the Deaf, who superseded the local mission, shut the centre about 1963 and the premises were knocked down shortly afterwards.

a prospect, around 1925, from the Bridgend Road corner of East Crawford Street looking westwards to Craigieknowes Street then Border Street and on towards its junction at the Victoria Bowling Green with Belville Street and Carwood Street.

The main building is Hillend School. Its design by H & D Barclay, the Glasgow architects, incorporated various beneficial features. Speaking tubes allowed direct communication between the headmaster's room and each classroom, double or overlapping stairs in a central hall gave separate access for the boys and girls to and from the upper floor while teachers could easily keep good discipline over all the pupils from any single location

James Watt Dock

Greenock Harbour Trust constructed the James Watt Dock during 1878–1886 to cope with the increasing size of ships and an ever growing amount of trade passing through the port. *City of Rome*, the passenger liner, was an iron ship of 8,453 tons built in 1881 by the Barrow Shipbuilding Company for the Inman Line. However, the shipping group refused to take delivery of the vessel which then served instead on Anchor Line services between Great Britain and the United States of America until broken up in Germany during 1903.

A Norwegian 3-masted barque is undergoing repairs. Among the other ships, a cargo freighter is coaling at the jetty. Different grades of coal were chosen by the engineers according to their requirements and then mixed together by a gang of stevedore trimmers as each kind was loaded into the vessel's bunkers.

The huge red brick warehouse, near the *City of Rome*, had some clever features including a bulk handling system whereby its hollow cast iron columns could be used to move grain, sugar or any other suitable bulk commodity between floors and then on to railway freight trains which ran on a track laid along the ground floor of the building. The James Watt Dock ceased being a major harbour with the advent of containerisation in the 1970s but still provides general mooring berths, a fisheries patrol vessel base and ship repairing facilities.

The *Minerva* and *Clan Macdougall* Collision

Local shipping activities during the morning of Monday, 12 November, 1906 presented a scene of bustling normality to observers. *Minerva* was a Glasgow & South Western Railway Company paddle steamer built in 1893 for summer excursions from Greenock to the Clyde Coast resorts and winter service between Ardrossan and Arran. She lay coaling at a riverside berth at the Albert Harbour.

Just after 9 o'clock, *Clan Macdougall*, a modern 4,710-ton cargo liner in Cayzer Irvine & Company Limited's Clan Line fleet, had a steering gear failure while bound from Glasgow to Liverpool and the Far East. The vessel swerved off course, hit the harbour quay wall and crashed into the port side of *Minerva*, grinding the 315-ton paddler against the stone dock wall. All the steamer's moorings were carried away. Crew members barely had time to leap ashore before *Clan Macdougall* turned their ship round and struck the starboard side of the little vessel as well. The heavily laden freighter, still with considerable way on, then forced the steamer along to Princes Pier.

Minerva suffered devastation but *Clan Macdougall* only had insignificant bow damage. Somehow there were no casualties on either vessel. Initially towed back to the Albert Harbour berth, *Minerva* was moored alongside a jetty in the Garvel Basin about 2 o'clock that afternoon – as seen in this view – before entering the Garvel Dry Dock for a survey. Repairs were carried out by the Clyde Shipbuilding & Engineering Company in Port Glasgow over several weeks. *Clan Macdougall 's* owners accepted liability for the incident. *Minerva* continued steamer sailings on the Clyde until requisitioned by the Admiralty in the First World War to serve as a Royal Navy auxiliary patrol vessel, before being broken up about 1927.

A Demonstration of a
Motor Sweeper Watering Wagon

In 1923, the Corporation of Greenock's Cleansing Committee decided to replace the cleansing department's old street cleaning lorry with a modern efficient vehicle. Bailie William Millar, Convener, and Councillor David McMillan, Vice-Convener, were remitted to attend the forthcoming Annual Conference and Exhibition of the Institute of Cleansing Superintendents in Aberdeen, assess the motor sweepers on display and arrange the procurement of tenders from various manufacturers. Soon afterwards, the town council approved the committee's recommendation to purchase a motor sweeper watering wagon from Laffly Schneider SA, a French manufacturer of service vehicles, through their subsidiary organisation, the Laffly (England) Company Limited. VS 1042 was delivered in the spring of the following year.

David McMillan and several other committee members, their officials, a Fire Brigade representative and a *Greenock Telegraph* journalist met at 2 o'clock on Wednesday, 12 March, 1924 for a demonstration of the vehicle at the local authority depot in Main Street. Easily driven and operated by one man, the chain-driven vehicle had a 24 HP petrol engine giving a top speed of 12 miles an hour. When sweeping, a 6 feet long brush covered the road surface right into the kerb and a supply of water directed just in front of it during dry weather prevented any dust rising into the air. For street washing, a regulated fine spray of water was projected with considerable force up to 30 feet on either side of the machine by two adjustable nozzles aimed at an angle to the ground, the impact moving every kind of dirt and refuse into the gutters. The committee members and the others expressed total satisfaction with the wagon and felt sure that it would be a great benefit to the community.

Later, an extensive *Greenock Telegraph* report duly appeared highlighting the Corporation of Greenock's position at the forefront of street cleaning practice in Great Britain.

Horse Trams

Local horse tram operations began in Greenock in 1873. The Vale of Clyde Tramways Company's service between Greenock and Gourock was immediately popular. Passengers were impressed with the smooth comfortable ride, so unlike a miserable bone-shaking journey on the earlier horse buses. Although it was planned to develop a network of routes, the idea was dropped because of the hilly terrain in the district.

The Greenock & Port Glasgow Tramways Company, however, opened a service to and from each town during 1889. On the inaugural trip, civic dignitaries travelled in two trams along the route at the invitation of the company directors. Everybody regarded this celebration as another landmark in the provision of public transport around the neighbourhood. Here, one of their splendid five windows type horse trams in red and cream livery and fitted with garden seats is seen travelling along Main Street on regular service in the 1890s. Maximum speed was about 10 miles an hour.

All the conductors felt very superior to colleagues still at work on the horse buses, sometimes yelling cruel remarks to them about their "old hen houses".

In 1893–1894, the Greenock & Port Glasgow Tramways Company took over the Vale of Clyde Tramway's adjacent operations, allowing through services between Port Glasgow, Greenock and Gourock. Timetable schedules were fulfilled very satisfactorily, apart from routine incidents of trams coming off the rails, horses refusing to do any work and minor accidents caused by cart drivers misjudging their distance from the cars. The horse trams disappeared from local streets with the introduction of electric tramcars during 1901.

Horse trams operated in Greenock, Gourock and Port Glasgow from 1873
until they were replaced by electric tramcars in 1901

Ross & Marshall's Shipbuilding Yard

The Ross & Marshall partnership, a union of Alexander Ross's lighterage and coal business with James Marshall's lighterage and stevedoring enterprise, began trading during 1872. Later expansion included ventures into salvage, transhipment of timber, the provision of fresh water to ships plus laying moorings. In 1897, the firm opened these premises on Main Street, among other shipyards between the Victoria Harbour and the James Watt Dock, for the construction and repair of their own cargo vessels. A slipway and dock facilities were located on either side of a jetty. There was a small engine shop. Around fourteen ships were built altogether.

Steel lighters, better known as puffers from the characteristic sound of early vessels, formed the basic output from the yard. *Lucullite*, a Forth & Clyde Canal trader able to carry 100 tons of cargo, entered service in 1899. A larger Crinan Canal type ship, *Warlight*, 135 tons and 87 feet long, followed during 1920. Steel and wood steam yachts were produced for the company's partners as well. *Meteorlight*, 30 tons, 61 feet in length and equipped with a 6 HP Ross & Marshall engine, was completed during 1898. In 1900, delivery took place of *Ixolite*, a 30-ton twin screw vessel, nicely designed and provided with high quality furnishings. *Roselight*, 31 tons, 57 feet long and fitted with a 4 HP builder's engine, appeared in 1903.

Around 1925, Ross & Marshall Limited sold the works to Scotts' Shipbuilding & Engineering Company Limited, who merged it with their Cartsdyke Dockyard. Scott Lithgow Limited, subsequent occupiers of the site, continued shipbuilding up to the 1980s.

Ross-shire, Barque

Scott & Company, a predecessor of Scott Lithgow limited, built *Ross-shire for* Thomas Law & Company's Shire Line at their Cartsburn Dockyard during 1891. Small vessels were moored along the far side of the ship when this photograph was taken from Gourock. *Ross-shire* was a fine steel 4-masted single deck barque of 2,257 tons, 290 feet in length, manned by only 30 men and capable of sailing at 15 knots in fair conditions with a fresh quartering wind. Barques of this type could be produced quite cheaply and operated more economically than contemporary steamships. So large numbers were commissioned by sailing ship owners in a final bid to compete with steam.

Captain Andrew Baxter, one of the owner's best masters, commanded *Ross-shire* for a long time on the trade routes between Great Britain, the United States of America, South America, Australia, India and Japan. Good passage times by the vessel included Greenock to San Francisco in 108 days and Calcutta to the Lizard in 103 days.

Under the command of Captain William Couper, while *Ross-shire* was loading saltpetre at Pisagua in Chile just before Christmas in 1900, fire broke out through carelessness or a wilful act by a member of the crew. Quickly ablaze, the ship became a total loss, sinking at the harbour moorings. All on board escaped to safety.

Greenock Foundry Company Engineers

These stalwart men were the Greenock Foundry Company's engineers around 1892. This firm began in the 1790s as Anthony Burrow & William Lawson's Iron and Brass Foundry making household goods and doing shipyard work. Quite soon, however, trade became difficult and the partnership was sold to Brownlie & Campbell, their main rivals. William Brownlie later took sole charge of the foundry. During 1825, John Scott & Sons, shipbuilders, purchased the business on realising that steamships would replace sailing vessels. As Scott Sinclair & Company, it then began the long history of marine engineering by the Scotts. In 1859, this industrial venture was renamed the Greenock Foundry Company and during 1904, to promote group development, the firm was absorbed into Scotts' Shipbuilding & Engineering Company Limited, latterly part of Scott Lithgow Limited. Closure took place in the 1980s. Trades group photographs such as this one were a common feature of shipyard life.

Launch of HMS *Ajax*

A 'King George V' class super-dreadnought battleship, HMS *Ajax*, had been ordered by the Admiralty for the Royal Navy in the 1910–1911 naval construction programme. The design comprised a steel vessel of 23,100 tons, 598 feet long, manned by around 900 men, carrying a main armament of 10 13.5-inch guns supported by various secondary weapons and equipped with Parsons turbine machinery developing 32,900 HP driving four propellers to give an endurance range of 4,060 miles at a speed of 18 knots or a top speed of 21 knots.

The launch on Thursday, 21 March, 1912 produced a carnival atmosphere in the town. All morning, crowds of sightseers converged on the shipyard. Vehicular traffic was heavy with a constant stream of motor cars, horse-drawn carriages and well-filled trams. Mounted and

foot policemen maintained order to ease the congestion. Numerous viewpoints on Belville Street and St Lawrence Street accommodated throngs of casual observers. The Victoria Harbour and Garvel Basin quays were also crammed with people. Hundreds of Scotts' workers, who had been given a holiday and entrance tickets, queued with their families and friends in long lines for admission at both yard gates. Inside, people hastily found their way to the best positions which were soon full to capacity. The massive hull of the warship dominated the scene while flags and bunting provided colourful surroundings. Popular melodies played by a band filled the air. Towards 1 o'clock, everybody watched the Duchess of Sutherland, the battleship's sponsor, arrive with her party at the launching platform, carrying a magnificent bouquet of flowers and escorted by Scotts' chairman, Charles Cunningham Scott. Following them were 400 official guests, many of whom had come on a special train from Glasgow to Greenock Central Station and then in private tramcars to the shipyard. The Reverend W J Nichol Service, minister of the West Kirk at once conducted the religious service held at the launch of naval vessels.

Then, amid increased tension, a signal was given to clear the ways. The Duchess then named the ship HMS *Ajax*, smashing a bottle of champagne on the bows. She also used ceremonial scissors with gold handles in the shape of dolphins to cut a cord, symbolically releasing the warship from the building berth. As the vessel slid gracefully into the water there were rousing cheers and the band played *God Save the King* followed by *Rule Britannia*. On the river, there was a fairly strong wind and tide, but the ship was safely taken in tow by four of the Clyde Shipping Company Limited's powerful tugs and moored in Scotts' shipyard fitting-out basin.

Afterwards, the crowds of spectators dispersed while the guests attended a formal luncheon in the joiners' shop transformed by artistic decorations for the occasion. Clear oxtail soup, galantine of chicken and truffles with a salad, almond creams and coffee was a typical menu selection from a choice of 26 dishes. Amid the toasts and speeches which concluded the proceedings, Charles Cunningham Scott presented a beautiful casket holding the launching scissors to the Duchess of Sutherland as a memento of the event.

Scotts' Shipbuilding & Engineering Company Limited completed this warship in 1913. During the First World War, HMS *Ajax* was in the Royal Navy's Grand Fleet and fought at the Battle of Jutland. The vessel was scrapped in 1927–1928.

A Fancy Dress Horse and Bicycle Parade

Promoters held this event to raise funds for the local Nursing Association – a supplier of voluntary medical care – during the afternoon of Saturday, 14 August, 1909 in Port Glasgow. These participants from Greenock and Gourock were travelling along Rue End Street and Main Street at Charing Cross, already collecting money in pots, pans and other receptacles, to the Five Lamps starting point where they joined Port Glasgow's group.

Near 3 o'clock, the 5th Battalion Argyll & Sutherland Highlanders (Territorials) Pipe Band led off the cavalcade at an easy pace around the central streets of the town. The pageant comprised 130 paraders with horses, horse-drawn carts or bicycles. When the column had reached the Five Lamps landmark again, a senior nurse presented almost 30 fancy dress prizes in various categories to the gathering.

Dockers and Cargo Handling

These dockers unloading a cargo of wool from the Ayr Steamship Company's iron coastal steamer *Amphion* at one of Greenock's riverside wharfs during the early 1890s depended on teamwork. Lumpers in each hold put the sacks into rope slings which were then hoisted out by colleagues using the steam winch operated derricks with hand signal guidance from hatchmen. The loads were dumped on a skid and the bags taken ashore to barrowmen for checking by samplers and weighers before being stowed in the dock sheds. Whenever necessary, tailors repaired any sacks which had been accidentally ripped open. Loading cargo aboard the ship was done in the same kind of way, but goods were lifted directly from the quayside into the holds without using skids. Upon completion of the job, sweepers-up made everything tidy.

Dockers toiled long hours each day, often from 8 o'clock in the morning until 10 o'clock at night, if cargo vessels like *Amphion* required a fast turn round in port. Inevitably, accidents such as men being hit by swinging derrick hooks were a common occurrence which sometimes resulted in fatalities. Greenock dockers had a fine reputation on Clydeside over many years for their skill at work.

David McEwing's Painting and Decorating Business

David McEwing started his business in Arthur Street about 1881, changing its location several times in the early years to other premises along this road. Here is the proprietor outside the shop at 7 Arthur Street around 1925 during a period of diversification as a general merchant. Clearly, it was a normal breezy day judging from the way his apron is blowing in the wind. In all likelihood, the neighbourhood beat policemen maintained a regular working acquaintance with him on their patrols. Or maybe they had heard of the presence of the photographer.

The Cartsburn Street and Arthur Street junction was familiarly known to everybody at this time as Cartsburn Corner. Some time later, David McEwing brought Peggy and May, his daughters, into the firm serving customers in the shop. Popular and helpful, they were a valuable asset. Many people kept returning with further work. When David McEwing retired, they took over control of the business, at one point even moving the premises to yet another site on Arthur Street, until it was closed down in the 1940s.

Ardgowan Distillery Fire

On the evening of Friday, 12 June, 1903 a fire broke out at the Ardgowan Distillery Company on Baker Street which was surrounded by a densely populated residential district and various industrial concerns. People gazing at the scene from houses around Lynedoch Street and Antigua Street watched as flames burst through the roof and climbed high into the sky. Since the fire was easily visible from many parts of the town, thousands of citizens gathered to watch events from Wellington Park, the surrounding roads and even West End viewpoints.

Hard worked police patrols and naval personnel kept control of the crowds. With the outbreak having a firm hold and the store containing an immense number of full whisky casks, it was pointless for the firefighters to attempt saving the place. Instead, they directed all their efforts on preventing the flames spreading to the distillery

building and properties nearby. Every floor of the warehouse was soon alight, generating intense heat. Consequently, the inhabitants of Baker Street and Ingleston Street tenements evacuated their houses, stacking personal articles in nearby roads for safety.

When the fire had been raging for three hours, the stone walls of the warehouse collapsed inwards with a crash producing a vast upsurge of flames. Burning liquor which had accumulated on the ground floor of the building escaped and set fire to the belongings. Suddenly, the whisky poured down Baker Street in a huge 3 or 4 inches deep torrent with flames climbing seven feet into the air. There was complete panic among the mass of residents and spectators in its path.

Just as the situation appeared to have been brought under control in the lower part of the thoroughfare, some blazing spirits found its way into a stream which supplied water to industrial works throughout the area. Greenock Foundry Company's finishing

Roxburgh Street Sugar Refinery Chimney Demolition

On the morning of Thursday, 8 April, 1909 thousands of spectators stood in Roxburgh Street and Holmscroft Street, on the roofs of adjoining properties and on the slopes of Prospecthill to watch the Roxburgh Street Sugar Refinery Company's chimney stalk, fully 160 feet high, being razed to the ground.

The photograph below shows spectators after the demolition.

shop almost burned down. Then, around 10 o'clock, there was an explosion at the Deerpark Grain Mill on East Stewart Street and Springkell Street caused by spontaneous combustion of flour dust heated as the fiery water swept through its wheelhouse. Part of the mill was blown into the road, the ruins being immediately aflame. Numerous bystanders watching the distillery from this spot were trapped in the wreckage.

Sadly, seven victims including 5-year old Christine Buchan died and six others had frightful injuries requiring hospital treatment. Meanwhile, although the main distillery building had been saved, there was colossal destruction of property. Some 800,000 gallons of whisky were lost as well. The Ardgowan Distillery Company blaze, undoubtedly, made a lasting impression on the community because it could have swept with ease through the whole East End area.

Queen Mary Day

(opposite)
Queen Mary off Greenock – her
first public sighting after leaving
John Brown's yard at Clydebank on
24 March 1936

Queen Mary was ordered by Cunard White Star Limited from John Brown & Company Limited, Clydebank in 1930 for their passenger sailings between Southampton and New York. Yard No 534 comprised a steel vessel of 80,774 tons, 1,019 feet long, capable of carrying 2,139 passengers, crewed by 1,101 people and equipped with turbine engines driving four screws to give a service speed of 29 knots. Construction soon began but stopped in 1931 when the Cunard Line encountered financial difficulties caused by economic recession at this time. Work eventually resumed during 1934, allowing the ship to be launched later that year for completion in the shipyard's fitting-out basin.

Public interest in the glamorous liner was immense. By 10 o'clock on the morning of Tuesday, 24 March, 1936 when *Queen Mary* left Clydebank for trials before entering service, crowds of people from all over the country were arriving in Greenock to join the local community for a glimpse of her. The London Midland & Scottish Railway Company ran many packed excursion trains over its vast route network and supplied highly popular frequent train services with cheap fares from Glasgow. Motor traffic reached an influx of some 1,500 vehicles an hour. Everyone learned that the vessel was coming downriver by a signal of exploding detonators at the Municipal Buildings. Soon afterwards, businesses suspended their activities to let workers join the commotion.

Sightseers first saw *Queen Mary* in the distance coming out of mist into bright sunshine just before 1 o'clock. An audible intaking of breath showed the astonishment of people when they realised the huge size of the Cunarder. Motor boats and yachts provided a wonderful escort. At the Corporation of Greenock's Inchgreen Gasworks, Provost J W Bell and 400 guests watched from a grandstand, everybody appreciating a running commentary on the ship's progress. Women newsreel operators there climbed the steps of a gasholder to record pictures. Downstream, a good-natured gathering of around 60,000 spectators on the Great Harbour embankment cheered and waved their handkerchiefs fervently in an impressive tribute as the vessel passed slowly along the channel. More crowds lined Custom House Quay.

Beside the Albert Harbour, the Glebe Sugar Refinery Company had 200 guests on a flat roof of the works. Thousands of schoolchildren and their teachers assembled on the waterfront, nearly complete obedience prevailing throughout this special outing. On Princes Pier, lucky spectators had a marvellous view from the railway station balcony over the throngs below on the wharf. Here, too, a small telephone exchange was installed with forty telephones for journalists from all over the world. A message in signal flags read 'Good luck' as *Queen Mary* proceeded towards the estuary. London Midland & Scottish Railway Company steamers at the quayside prepared to sail on continuous 1-hour trips round the liner. Along the Esplanade, 50,000 spectators stood about 12 deep, many carrying a camera and binoculars. Greenock Motor Services operated a special bus service every 7 minutes from George Square to the top of the Lyle Hill. There, more gatherings of awestruck sightseers compared the size of the giant vessel with numerous town buildings. Crowds at the Battery Park, reminiscent of a Fair Saturday, mainly comprised elderly people and parents with young children because there was less risk of bystanders being crushed in its wide open spaces.

Dramatically, *Queen Mary* arrived at the Tail of the Bank just after 2 o'clock to a welcome by a chorus of hornblowing from ships at the anchorage, the accompanying small craft and motorists on the waterfront. It was reckoned that during this memorable day nearly 250,000 people saw the liner from Greenock.

Once in service, the Cunarder captured the Blue Riband for the fastest crossings of the Atlantic Ocean and became especially popular with American people. The liner was requisitioned by the Admiralty in the Second World War, serving as a troop transport. After an overhaul, *Queen Mary* resumed the passenger sailings between Southampton and New York in 1947 but air travel soon attracted people away from regular ocean voyages. During 1967, the ship was sold to the City of Long Beach in the United States of America and now serves as a maritime tourist attraction.

King Edward in the East India Dry Dock

Clyde steamers were regularly overhauled by James Lamont & Company Limited, shipbuilders and shiprepairers, in the East India Dry Dock. *King Edward*, the first merchant ship in the world with turbine engines, is seen here undergoing maintenance work around 1906–1910. *King Edward* was built in 1901 by William Denny & Brothers Limited, Dumbarton for the Turbine Steamer Syndicate, a partnership specially formed to demonstrate the practicality of this propulsion system in a commercial vessel by John Williamson, the river steamer owner; the Dennys and the Parsons Marine Stream Turbine Company Ltd.

The ship, allocated to the route between Greenock and Campbeltown, was an immediate success with a speed of more than 20 knots – faster than any paddle boat – and a passenger capacity of 1,966 people. Short evening cruises with music on board were also popular. In 1902, transferred to Turbine Steamers Limited ownership, the vessel was placed on the Greenock to Inverary run. During the First World War, *King Edward* mostly served as a troop transport in the English Channel, but also worked as a hospital ship on a round voyage to Archangel. Sailings, thereafter, again took place between Greenock and Campbeltown with occasional periods serving the Inverary route. Taken over by Williamson-Buchanan Steamers Limited during 1927, trips were operated from Glasgow to Rothesay incorporating optional excursions to Arran, and later Loch Striven, the Kyles of Bute and around Great Cumbrae.

King Edward was acquired by the Caledonian Steam Packet Company Limited in 1935, being passed to a subsidiary venture for several years and then rejoining the main Caledonian Steam Packet Company Limited fleet. The ship continued working on the normal long distance routes with a cruise from Glasgow to Lochgoilhead featuring at weekends as well. Duties as a ferry and shipping tender around the Clyde were carried out in the Second World War. Afterwards, this steamer sailed on the Glasgow to Tighnabruaich and Arran coast excursion runs. *King Edward* was scrapped in 1952 by the West of Scotland Shipbreaking Company Limited, Troon.

King Edward, the first merchant ship in
the world to have turbine engines,
operated for half a century on the Clyde

Custom House and Beacon Fountain

One of the principal Custom Houses on Clydeside, this magnificent building was constructed in 1817–1819 to a classical design by William Burn, an eminent Scottish architect. Evidently, most of the men in the labour force had been soldiers in the Napoleonic Wars. Facing northwards across Custom House Quay, previously known as Steamboat Quay, it was the Customs & Excise centre for Greenock's thriving overseas trade with the United States of America, Canada, the West Indies and elsewhere. Special features include the Long Room with its enormous wooden counter, almost 40 feet in length, where merchants, shipowners and sea captains oversaw the necessary administration of their daily business. Until the establishment of shipping exchanges, it was also a suitable central meeting place for their general discussions on commercial matters. Another highlight, is the fine Georgian staircase in the main hall. These days, the Custom House contains the Greenock VAT Office, the National Centre for Gaming Machine Licences and a Customs & Excise Museum and Exhibition.

The tall cast-iron Beacon Fountain, standing in front of the Custom House, provides a striking focal point on Custom House Quay. This unusual Corinthian column was designed in 1868 by William Clark, a highly-admired local marine artist. Amazingly, it features a shipping beacon, a clock, a weather vane, drinking fountains, a fog bell, and a postbox. Greenock's coat of arms is also displayed on the column. It was made by Rankin & Blackmore, local marine engineers and is an elegant reminder of former times.

The Custom House photographed in the 1960s

East Quay Lane

East Quay Lane originally served the major harbour built in 1707–1710 to ensure the community won a fair share of the maritime trading opportunities arising from the Union of Scotland and England. Later, once the town had grown bigger, it linked Cathcart Street and Steamboat Quay, later known as Custom House Quay, passing alongside this dock which had become the West Harbour.

During the early 1800s, many of the folk living and working in the lane had colourful personalities – Elizabeth Halliday, 'Pie Betty' ran a successful pastry shop chiefly because gentlemen found her as much a lure as the merchandise. The lane later degenerated into a notorious unsavoury passage of

bars, shebeens and other premises which people had to pass on their way from the Caledonian Railway Company's Cathcart Street Station to the river steamers at the quayside. Sailors were often engaged in bar room brawls and stabbings. Robbery was common at all times of the day.

In the 1860s, Greenock Corporation held discussions with the railway company about improving the situation by widening the street and building a covered shopping arcade. Nothing, however, came of the idea. Ultimately, East Quay Lane was replaced by Brymner Street on redevelopment of the district in 1877–1878.

Upper Greenock Station Railway Disaster

About 4 o'clock in the afternoon of Thursday, 11 July, 1907 a Caledonian Railway Company freight train left Upper Greenock Station Depot carrying goods for delivery to Overton Paper Mill on the hillside behind the town. Its crew were all East End people. Edward Steel was the driver with William McEwan as his fireman and Robert Scott working as the brakesman. All went well until the saddle tank locomotive and three wagons reached the Old Largs Road level crossing. Here, the train stopped while Scott got off to open the gates. Its brakes, however, would not hold and it began travelling back down the steep incline at an ever increasing speed. Frantically, the brakesman attempted to halt the runaway with a sprag but success proved impossible. Concerned about helping the driver in some way, he then jumped on a wagon but realised that a serious accident was inevitable and leapt off again. In slight discomfort from a tumble on landing, he ran headlong down the hill after the others. Bravely, Edward Steel and William McEwan manned their posts on the engine footplate until catastrophe was quite unavoidable before jumping to the ground.

The little train, moving at an incredible pace, hit siding buffers near the station with tremendous force, leapt high in the air, fell on its side, ploughed its way over an embankment, jumped a small burn and landed on the Wellington Bowling Green road. One wagon remained in its position behind the locomotive, the others being scattered elsewhere. Coming upon the scene, Robert Scott was particularly horrified to find the driver lying crumpled against the buffers. Sadly, Edward Steel sustained terrible injuries and died very soon after his admission to Greenock Infirmary. Steel, a highly respected 60-year old widower living with his daughter, had served with the Caledonian Railway Company for over forty years and was regarded as a conscientious train driver. Over the next day, a breakdown gang removed the wrecked engine to Ladyburn Railway Works for repair and returned the almost undamaged goods wagons to Upper Greenock Station Depot. Crowds of townspeople visited the scene of this disaster, it becoming a general topic of conversation for some time afterwards.

Neill Dempster & Neill, Sugar Refiners

John Neill and Duncan F Dempster, relatives, founded this business as Neill & Dempster in 1853. Their 7-floor cane sugarhouse was situated on Dellingburn Street beside another sugar refinery. Trading was very successful allowing enlargement of the premises within a few years. In 1863, the firm became Neill Dempster & Neill when John Neill's son, also called John Neill, joined the partnership – he is accompanied by Jura in the picture during later life. Misfortune, however, abruptly struck the venture in 1865. Fire destroyed the sugar refinery, 100 men losing their jobs. Instead of erecting new premises, the partners acquired the cotton mill on Drumfrochar Road and carried on the cotton spinning business for a couple of years. About 1868, they decided to return to sugar refining and built a new cane sugarhouse in the lower part of the cotton mill grounds – the photograph shows these large works from Mearns Street. Profits soon rose to outstanding levels. In the 1870s, John Neill the younger, invented and patented a pressing machine to improve the production of lump, loaf or block sugar. This allowed these three types of sugar to be made easily in any form or size and brought great savings in time, labour and floor space. When the founders, John Neill and Duncan Dempster, retired, company management was continued by John Neill, the son, several other members of the Neill family and another Duncan F Dempster, yet one more son named after his father. The collapse of the business in 1924 resulted from severe price competition with foreign sugar refineries and a prolonged strike by the local sugar industry's workforce.

Wellpark Parish Church's Junior Choir

Wellpark Parish Church on Regent Street was built to a rather plain design by Paisley architects, Rennison & Scott, in 1877–1879. Its members came from the East End and the surrounding central areas of the town.

Somewhere around the 1920s, parents in the congregation eagerly acquired copies of this picture showing the children's choir members in *The Magic Ruby*, a moralising cantata, along with William Dickson, their conductor, outside the church doorway.

Their church later became Wellpark West Church. During 1996 it united with the Mid Kirk in Cathcart Square to form the Wellpark Mid Kirk.

Baron Bailie's House

During the 1630s, John Shaw, Greenock's laird, obtained a crown charter giving the community the rights of a burgh of barony. Privileges including the establishment of the town as a freeport and the authority to hold a weekly market and two annual fairs made it a centre of some economic and social importance. This situation meant that local government was controlled by the laird who naturally appointed a chief administrator, the baron bailie, to act as his representative in the community. The baron bailie had responsibilities covering law and justice, tax, weights and measures, the minister's stipend, maintenance of the church, the schoolmaster's salary, poor relief assessment, repairing the town clock and the administration of the Shaw family's estate. Consequently, it was sensible that his house should be near the laird's mansion – this site eventually lay on the hillside below the Wellpark which was created from the mansion grounds around the time of its demolition in the 1800s. Through new charters granted by Sir John Shaw during 1741 and 1751 in a farsighted liberal action, this system of municipal management was replaced by a town council appointed annually by the feuars and sub-feuars. However, the position continued with the council which comprised 2 baron bailies, 1 treasurer and 6 councillors. Since the council had corporate authority to regulate the public finances, make rules and laws, keep public order, hold a weekly or more frequent court, imprison or otherwise punish wrongdoers and admit merchants or tradesmen as burgesses, the role of the baron bailie was a much less powerful one. This system was formally abolished by the Reform Act of 1832 which provided a democratic system of government by popular election. The baron bailie's house, latterly just an office building, became a washhouse for residents of adjacent tenements on Cathcart Street until the 1930s, lay abandoned from then on gradually turning into a ruin and was demolished in the 1960s.

Elevenses in McArthur's Luncheon & Tea Rooms

McArthur's Luncheon Rooms and Tea Rooms on Cathcart Street
opened about 1900, being popular at once with many townspeople.
Here sugar industry businessmen and their associates have found
respite from dealings at the nearby Greenock Sugar Exchange during
1909. John Barnhill Walker, seated at the left-hand table, was a
partner with the major local sugar refining firm of John Walker &
Company which traded for over 150 years. At the extreme right of the
picture, Duncan F D Neill was a partner in Neill Dempster & Neill,
another Greenock sugar refining company. A keen yachtsman, he
became Sir Thomas Lipton's "honest and straightforward" America's
Cup yachting adviser. Charles G Fulton, in the foreground, was a
partner with the insurance broking company of MacIntyre & Fulton,
Glasgow. Later, he was also made a director of P MacCallum & Sons,
the prominent metal merchants and shipowners in Greenock. Sitting
below the calendar, D Graham Ramsay worked for J V Drake &
Company, sugar merchants in Exchange Buildings. Donald
MacDonald, just visible on the left hand side, was a sugar broker with
MacDonald Hutcheson & Company on Cathcart Street. The other
gentlemen were John McCulloch and Hedley Lyle. McArthur's
Luncheon Rooms and Tea Rooms closed in 1928, sadly missed by
patrons.

Cathcart Street

The view on the previous page shows the street about 1930 when,
unlike today, it was the commercial centre of the town. Premises
included banks; Greenock Sugar Exchange; Thomas Black & Sons
Limited, sailmakers and shipchandlers; Fyfe & Murray and other
insurance offices; Lindsay & Crookston Limited, a coal merchant; J & J
Denholm Limited, among numerous shipping offices; hotels; the Head
Post Office and shops like Smith's Warehouse. Cathcart Street Hall had
seating capacity for 150 people. In addition, the London, Midland &
Scottish Railway Company's Greenock Central Station was nearby. The
Gourock Pullman Motor Services Company bus, HS 4851, an
Associated Daimler in blue and cream livery, was operating on a public
service between Gourock and Glasgow. Further away, the Mid Kirk,
originally the New Parish Church and now the Wellpark Mid Kirk,
dominates its surroundings. Built during 1759–1761 with the steeple
being completed in 1787, table pew accommodation is provided for
1,600 worshippers. Its facade was constructed with high quality local
sandstone and modelled on the front elevation of St Martin's-in-the-
Fields Church, London.

William Quarrier's Home

A house in this tenement on Cross Shore Street was the birthplace of William Quarrier, founder of Quarrier's Homes, in 1829 – the entrance was through the stone archway. It was home until his father, a ship's carpenter, died of cholera in 1834. Mother and children then moved to Glasgow where they could maintain a living by fine sewing. There, just seven years old, Quarrier entered a pin factory as a hand machine operator. Later, he became a shoemaker. Quarrier easily obtained work in a local shop, taking up Christianity at the same time. At 20, he acquired his own premises and soon opened further outlets. Wealth allowed him to marry but his early hardships combined with the poverty encountered at work made him resolve to use his profits to assist poor and destitute children.

In 1864, William and others founded the Industrial Brigade Home in the Trongate with unlucky youngsters forming companies of newsvendors, shoeblacks and parcel boys. This venture, however, soon closed down. His attention turned instead to the formation of orphan homes in Glasgow, all of them being a great success. Numerous Destitute Children's Emigration Homes sent youngsters to Canada where receiving centres placed each child with a suitable family. Dovehill Night Refuge & Mission Hall carried out its own work with children and at the James Morrison Street City Home, boys

learnt a trade and girls were trained in house-keeping. Thereafter, national childcare provision took over Quarrier's life.

In 1876–1878, the Orphan Homes of Scotland village was built midway between Bridge of Weir and Kilmacolm. Before long, there were over fifty houses laid out like a normal community with church, shop, laundry, hospital, school, post office, farm, workshop and other facilities. Each home ran on a family system with a 'father' and a 'mother' to supervise around thirty children in each cottage. Tuberculosis sanatoriums and homes for epileptics were constructed on adjoining ground. It was a model of residential care far ahead of its period.

When Quarrier died in 1903, management of the institution was carried on by the family with advice from influential trustees. Eventually, the trustees took sole control of its administration, gradually introducing more involvement with the local community in areas like education and hospital facilities. Quarrier's Homes became the formal name of the organisation.

When the Cross Shore Street tenement was demolished in 1929 – the centenary of Quarrier's birth – its archway entrance was rebuilt as the Quarrier's Homes War Memorial.

Longwell Close

Longwell Close began its existence as a narrow street passage with just a few houses around 1680. By the 1780s, there having been considerable town growth, it ran between Cathcart Street and Shaw Street, now the eastern section of Dalrymple Street. One of numerous similar lanes in the vicinity, it contained the 50–60 feet deep Long Well which for a long time supplied people with cool spring water of a particularly good quality – often used as an essential ingredient in punch and other drinks consumed by citizens patronising the neighbourhood taverns. This photograph illustrates very well how the passage, along with its surroundings, gradually degenerated into a slum quarter during the 1800s, with as many as 1600 people eventually occupying each acre of land. The poles jutting out across the alley were supports for hanging everyday washing out to dry. In 1877–1878, on reconstruction of the locality, Longwell Close was replaced by Duff Street.

Anchor Inn

The Anchor Inn was reputedly built in 1703, a large ornate edifice on the coastal highway through Greenock surpassing most of the adjacent premises in looks. When more development of the town had taken place, the stretch of road on which it lay was called Shaw Street, now replaced by the eastern part of Dalrymple Street. The leading hotel in this community for a long period, popular with affluent visitors like sea captains, it eventually faced competition from other high class establishments such as the Museum Hotel on William Street and the Tontine Inn on Cathcart Street.

During the 1800s, however, its respectability declined along with the neighbouring district into squalor. When the hotel closed, the place was used for various purposes. This picture shows the Anchor Inn building being demolished in 1877–1878 during clearance of the Shaw Street area to facilitate renovation work. One eminent West End gentleman collected a few beautiful architectural ornaments such as those on the roof of the premises to decorate his garden summerhouse.

Town Centre Slum Tenement Housing

Acting under the provisions of the Housing (Scotland) Act 1930, the Corporation of Greenock held an inquiry during 1931 into living conditions in the town centre around Church Place, Hamilton Street, Market Street, Manse Lane, Smith's Lane and the Vennel. The area had developed haphazardly over many years producing grim congestion and overcrowding. Poverty aggravated the situation, even if most residents tried to maintain reasonable standards of cleanliness. Further incentive for clearing the slums was provided by eminent townspeople giving the local

authority financial support on condition that work proceeded rapidly. This tenement at 7 Market Street, seen from its backcourt, was a typical property. Many of the buildings, some 175 years old, showed dreadful signs of age and disrepair such as broken or sagging ceilings. Poor natural ventilation and serious limitations in sunlight were commonplace. Sanitary facilities, too, were extremely inadequate. Out of the 630 houses in this district, just two had baths, none had hot water and in some cases a WC served seven or eight large families. At other premises, 125 occupants had

access to their homes by a single common stair with no washing facilities. In addition, there was considerable rat and bug infestation. These conditions alongside widespread use of the traditional concealed or built-in bed, unsurprisingly, encouraged tuberculosis to such an extent that there was no other area in the town where it was more prevalent. Subsequently, Greenock Corporation obtained a Compulsory Clearance Order for the area, despite strong objections from some property owners, which resulted in the demolition and reconstruction of the area during the later 1930s.

The Volunteer Submarine Miners' Camp Parade

As 9 o'clock struck on the morning of Thursday, 6 July, 1893 the Greenock Company of the Clyde Volunteer Division, Royal Engineers, Submarine Miners – responsible for coastal defence minelaying across the river during wartime – paraded in review order at Cathcart Square for the march to their annual 15-day training camp beside Fort Matilda. Captain W W B Rodger, Divisional Commander, was in charge of the inspection with Captain Duncan F D Neill, better known as a Neill Dempster & Neill sugar refinery partner, in command of the local company. From a possible 63 volunteers, 60 men comprising two officers, two sergeants and fifty six rank and file soldiers fell in on the parade.

Construction of the Victoria Tower

A view of the Victoria Tower, Municipal Buildings nearing completion in the 1880s. Fireproof accommodation was originally provided on its first five floors to store the town records. Still a tremendous landmark nowadays, its extravagant 245 feet height plainly demonstrates Greenock's considerable wealth in Victorian times.

Diamond Jubilee Bar

For much of the 1800s and in the early 1900s, many of Greenock's public houses were clustered around the harbour area to capture the passing traffic with the Highlands and Ireland. Opened in 1897, the Diamond Jubilee Bar – its name loyally marking Queen Victoria's sixtieth year as a monarch – was situated on the western side of Manse Lane at its junction with Hamilton Street, near the Municipal Buildings. It is seen here in or about 1905. Closure took place by 1923. The proliferation of bars in Greenock at this time caused a widespread heavy drinking social problem, eventually relieved by temperance movement activities.

Smillie & Robson's, Model T Ford Lorry

William Smillie and John Robson founded their business as wholesale and retail fruit, flower and vegetable merchants about 1881.

A green Ford Model T 1.5-ton lorry, VS 851, bought during the 1910s, soon became very familiar to people around the town. Good handling characteristics, high body clearance from the ground to avoid damage caused by uneven road surfaces, robust suspension and simple maintenance made an ideal vehicle. This view shows John Robson in the lorry outside his home at Crindledyke, 62 Brisbane Street, Greenock when it was carrying a barrel of apples or potatoes and a wreath frame propped against the tailboard.

Smillie & Robson's business ceased trading around 1938.

Hamilton Street Neighbourhood

This is the Hamilton Street, Sugarhouse Lane, Westburn Street and West Blackhall Street corner of the town centre in 1897 when the Greenock & Port Glasgow Tramways Company operated a frequent horse tram service through the area on their route between Port Glasgow, Greenock and Gourock. Among the shops on Hamilton Street, the main commercial thoroughfare from the 1760s, were James McKelvie & Sons, booksellers and stationers; Alexander Millar, a pawnbroker; Brand & Mollison, launderers; Matthew Watson, the hairdresser; Thomas J Lipton and Cooper & Company, grocers; Morton & Kidd, the ironmongers; Francis Bleakley, tobacconist and Barr & Macfarlane, fleshers. As well as its normal daily public routine, Yielder's Cafe catered for wedding receptions, dances and other special functions.

Sugarhouse Lane, which crossed Hamilton Street at the restaurant, obtained its name through the first sugar refineries in the town being constructed at the top and bottom of this road in the 1700s. Premises in the lane were occupied by Richard Smith, a lemonade manufacturer; John Campbell, spirit dealer; Thomas Briton, glazier, carver and gilder; Dugald Cameron, auctioneers and Alexander Barr, a saddler.

Westburn Street's name is derived from the Westburn, once a major stream flowing through the district. Its estuary provided a harbour for local fishermen while various industries including a sailcloth factory, soapworks, a distillery, glueworks, cooperages and a dyeworks became established on its banks. During 1897, various businesses were trading on the street like William Ferguson, an ironmonger, gasfitter and tinsmith; Charles Cowley, shoemaker and J Wink & Company, cabinetmakers and upholsterers.

West Blackhall Street, adjacent, was a particularly good shopping centre at this time. Among the many retailers were Adam Alexander, an umbrella maker; Thomas Mackay, the baker; R & A Urie, china merchants; Laurie & Harley, milliners; John Forbes, a musicseller; Mitchell Hodge & Sons, house furnishers; Robert Love, an optician and William Shepherd & Company, bicycle, wringer and sewing machine dealers.

Launch of *Medina*

The P&O Steam Navigation Company Limited's order in 1910 for a passenger ship from Caird & Company Limited specified a 12,350-ton 'M' class ocean liner, 550 feet long carrying up to 670 passengers, crewed by 400 people and fitted with two quadruple expansion engines driving twin screws to produce a speed of over 16 knots. Design features aboard *Medina* included all the accommodation being located above the main deck for a comfortable life in tropical seas, interior furnishings much superior to anything previously seen on long-distance passenger ships, hydraulic cranes to provide noiseless cargo handling and even dishwashers of the latest type in the galley. Marconi radio equipment was also stipulated in the contract.

Medina, Yard No 317, was named just prior to 12 o'clock on Tuesday, 14 March, 1911 in bright springtime weather by Lady Alice Shaw Stewart. Sir Hugh Shaw Stewart, Provost W B McMillan, Patrick T Caird who was Caird's Chairman, the Reverend Thomas Lennie, P&O officials and over fifty local business people were among the launching party guests in the shipyard. Many sightseers witnessed the proceedings from close quarters beside the ceremonial platform while crowds of other folk stood at vantage points along the riverside from Princes Pier to Custom House Quay.

On completion, later that year, this passenger liner had a high profile in public affairs. Requisitioned as a royal yacht, the ship took King George V and Queen Mary on their state visit to India. Early in 1912, *Medina* was refitted by Caird & Company before entering P&O's Australian service and European cruise programmes. Like the other fine 'M' class ships, the vessel soon became very popular with travellers. Unluckily, the ship was torpedoed and sunk by a German submarine off Start Point in the English Channel during World War I.

Old West Kirk

Greenock's familiar Old West Kirk, built in 1589–1591, has always been a distinctive community landmark. At first called the Kirk of Greenock or the Parish Church of Wester Greenock, it stood on an impressive riverside site incorporating a graveyard which overlooked the entrance to the Westburn. For 175 years, this building was the only local place of worship until the New Parish Church, now the Wellpark Mid Kirk, was erected in the town centre. It then became the Old Parish Church, later still being renamed the West Parish Church. People, of course, just called it the Old West Kirk.

By 1837, the building was in poor structural condition and had become too small for the increasing number of worshippers attending services. The West Kirk, now St Luke's Church, was accordingly constructed as a replacement and when the congregation moved there in 1841, the earlier property lay abandoned with an uncertain future. During 1864, however, the West Parish Church was put back into good order and opened again, despite almost having become completely tumbledown. Thereafter, it was officially redesignated the North Parish Church but most folk carried on using the Old West Kirk name.

By World War I, its position at the bottom of Nicolson Street was almost enclosed by Caird & Company's shipbuilding yards, squalid tenements and ramshackle warehouses. Harland & Wolff Limited, who purchased Caird's business in 1916, realised that to construct large modern vessels, it was necessary to extend their works by having the adjacent properties including the church and its kirkyard grounds cleared away. Negotiations about the matter between Harland & Wolff, the Corporation of Greenock, Greenock Presbytery and the Old West Kirk over several years eventually reached a settlement in 1924. Harland & Wolff undertook to present the church authorities with a new site on the Esplanade, demolish the old place of worship and rebuild it incorporating another design of steeple on the replacement location. They also agreed to erect a parochial hall in the grounds and lay out another kirkyard incorporating gravestones from the original church lands.

Demolition took place during 1925–1926 when Harland & Wolff were constructing *Rawalpindi* and *Rajputana*, passenger liners for the P&O's Bombay and Far East service. The church was then rebuilt on the new site in 1926–1928. Afterwards it was formally renamed the Old West Kirk at last. Quadricentennial anniversary celebrations took plae in 1991.

(opposite)
the Old West Kirk with Harland & Wolff's shipyard encroaching in the background

(bottom, left)
the church and its graveyard on the original sight

(bottom, right)
town development surrounding the Old West Kirk

(top)
rebuilding the Old West Kirk at the
new site on the Esplanade

(bottom)
the workforce who demolished and
reconstructed the Old West Kirk

(opposite)
the Old West Kirk on the Esplanade
shortly after its reopening around 1928

Hippodrome

The Hippodrome – originally the Theatre Royal then the Palace Music Hall and a brief spell as the Pavilion – in West Blackhall Street near Grey Place was a favourite theatre with many local people. It opened in 1908 with a variety show featuring performances by Barton & Ashley, comedians; Gustave Fasola, the magician; Sibb & Sibb, clever trapeze artists; a dromoscope picture show; Jack Neil, a Scottish comedian; The McConnell Trio and Frances Letty, a "coon singer and dancer". Musical accompaniment was provided by the Hippodrome Orchestra.

Numerous comparable stagings, of course, followed over the years. In addition, pantomimes like *Mother Hubbard*, *Little Tommy Tucker* starring May Milby and *Sinbad the Sailor* regularly appeared during winter seasons. Families often had to queue for an hour or more to attend these productions promoted as "whirlwinds of laughter". Musicals at the Hippodrome such as *A Trip to Paris* and *The Silver Wedding* were always charming events. During 1909, the Greenock Amateur Operatic Company staged the comic opera *Nell Gwynne* in aid of local charities with Marguerite Fowler, a vivacious soprano singer, leading the rest of the cast. Later on, the John Riding Grand Opera Company productions of condensed operas including Giuseppe Verdi's *Rigoletto*, Sir Julius Benedict's *Lady of Killarney*, and W Vincent Wallace's *Maritana* all played to big houses. In 1912, *Loss of the Titanic*, an artistic myriorama with mechanical effects, quickly moved its audiences to tears.

Plays were another very significant part of the bill. Jimmie Learmouth starred in *Flyaway's Derby*, an incredible sketch with Newmarket racehorses performing on a revolving stage racetrack which travelled at fifty miles an hour. Naturally, crowds of people attended the Hippodrome on its last day in 1923 when Arthur Hinton and Peggy Courteney starred in excellent performances of *Motherhood*, a play set in contemporary times.

The Hippodrome was demolished in 1930. Statues on the building's facade representing Drama, Tragedy and Comedy – which originally adorned the Theatre Royal, Dunlop Street in Glasgow – were moved to ornament the Auchmountain Glen leisure area in the East End of the town.

Celebrating the Bicentenary of the Union

This anniversary commemoration of the Union of Scotland and England in 1707 organised by the Greenock Scottish Rights Association – a pressure group supporting political unity but which sought a fairer deal through federal government – began about 3 o'clock on the afternoon of Saturday, 4 May, 1907 in George Square. John Arnot, President of the Scottish Rights Association, chaired the event from an improvised stage accompanied by over forty dignitaries. 2,000 other people filled the surrounding area. Flags and bunting supplied bright decorations, Union Jacks and Scottish Standards being in conspicuous positions. George Square Baptist Church, built during 1888, loomed over the scene.

John Arnot briefly promoted his organisation and its campaign for parliamentary devolution in a well-received speech. He then presented two cast iron benches commemorating the union to the Greenock Ramblers' Club amid loud cheers. This presentation was followed by the choir giving a spirited rendering of *Scots Wha Hae* with band accompaniment which received tumultuous applause from the crowd. A resolution reaffirming support for the union, carried with tremendous acclamation, closed the meeting.

A View from Peat Road

A panorama, early in 1908, looking over Cowdenknowes Dam and the houses on Murdieston Street at the town centre and Helensburgh on the opposite bank of the Clyde. Initial development of Cornhaddock and Cowdenknowes – mostly Greenock Corporation's large housing schemes – took place during the 1920s and 1930s. The Peat Road area underwent development from then until the 1960s.

Lying furthest out at the Tail of the Bank, Greenock's famous anchorage, *Wyreema*, a 6,338-ton passenger ship and cargo liner, was newly built by Alexander Stephen & Sons Limited of Glasgow for the Australasian United Steam Navigation Company Limited, London and Sydney.

For many years this scene was very familiar to members of the Greenock Ramblers's Club and other hikers on country walks to Corlic Hill, Loch Thom, Shielhill Glen and elsewhere. People still enjoy the landscape from this spot.

Orangefield

This district takes its name from *Orangefield*, a mansion built at the start of urban development in the area during the early 1800s for John Wilson, a prosperous local grocer. Apparently, his friends found the house smelled rather strongly of the shop. It was demolished in the 1930s prior to the construction of St Patrick's Church on the site. Here is a 1907 illustration of Orangefield – looking from Brachelston Street towards Greenock West Station – which shows Burnside Dairy, adjoining the West Burn, beside Thomas McLelland's impressive Orangefield Baptist Church, opened in 1877.

Cowdenknowes

Cowdenknowes was just farmland until the Scottish Veterans' Garden City Association constructed six houses during 1920 for local former World War I servicemen. The Corporation of Greenock then built 204 homes over the next few years to relieve a shortage of housing in the town. This late 1920s prospect looking along Dunlop Street shows most of the completed development with the neighbouring Combination Prison for Renfrew, Argyll and Bute, nowadays HM Prison Greenock, standing out in the background.

Grieve Road Skyscrapers

Construction of Arran Court, Bute Court and Cumbrae Court – the first multistorey blocks of flats built for the Corporation of Greenock – began during 1962. Work proceeded so well, apart from some difficulty with the foundation borings, that occupancy took place in 1964. Their original tenants mostly comprised people relocated from mediocre dwellings or overcrowded accommodation in the East End, Drumfrochar Road/Mill Street and Peat Road parts of the town. Flittings into the three skyscrapers were carried out like a military operation by limiting the scope of activity to the flats on a single floor of each building in turn every day over twelve weeks and working from the top level downwards.

Everybody was thrilled with their pioneering new lifestyle in brickfaced tower blocks 134 feet high with 90 homes on 15 floors and service facilities including laundries, hobbies rooms, telephone kiosks, refuse rooms, stores and garages provided at ground level plus a sheltered clothes drying area on the roof. The all-electric flats comprising a kitchen, a living room, two bedrooms, a bathroom and a balcony – which gave an emergency exit to the house next door in the event of fire – were considered to be bright with a well-designed layout. Underfloor heating was an enormous benefit for everybody. As well as the normal conditions of council tenancy, there were supplementary rules about living in the buildings like a ban on loitering in public areas and a need for discretion over utilising the general refuse room waste chutes at early or late times of the day. Caretakers were also appointed to supervise each skyscraper. With the passing years, of course, alterations have taken place to the buildings and their associated services. All the facades of the blocks are now refurbished with metal cladding to stop rainwater penetration damaging the houses. Outdoor leisure facilities for children such as their jungle playing area have been superseded by a ball games court and a small adventure playground. More significantly, a new community centre has been built for the residents of the skyscrapers and people living in the vicinity.

Gateside Hospital

Gateside Hospital, initially Greenock & District Combination Hospital, was opened in 1908 to provide medical care for people suffering infectious diseases. This view from Overton, around 1913, shows its completely isolated position.

The administrative block with staff accommodation and a kitchen was situated at the centre of a group of separate fever pavilions within the grounds. Each pavilion had wards for the treatment of a particular infectious disease – typhus, diphtheria, measles, scarlet fever, tuberculosis, pneumonia and others. The scarlet fever pavilion also had separate buildings for the observation of doubtful cases, isolation of cases of double infection and convalescent treatment of patients before their discharge. Hospital telephones were connected to the public telecommunications system and regular anonymous identity number bulletins in the *Greenock Telegraph* identifying each patient as being 'serious', 'sharply ill', 'comfortable', 'same', 'improving', 'stable' and so on enabled families and friends to monitor the progress of people.

Gateside Hospital closed in 1979 when it was incorporated into Inverclyde Royal Hospital.

Princes Pier

Princes Pier, originally known by other names such as Albert Pier and West End Pier, was constructed in 1862–1870 with a Glasgow & South Western Railway Company subsidiary opening a station on the site during the same period.

This 1870s view from the western extremity of the pier shows the boat harbour and the area at the bottom of Campbell Street. It is likely that the brick building was used for Customs & Excise purposes. On the left side, a pavilion – linked to the railway station by a covered passage – provided steamer passengers with sheltered accommodation before they embarked on the vessels. The large shed, to the right, was a rafters' boathouse. Rafters, working in the timber trade, floated cargoes of logs brought to Greenock from Canada into storage ponds located all along the riverside for seasoning by the salt water. Afterwards, they redistributed them in the same way for use by local shipbuilding companies and timber merchants. One of their 14-oared pulling boats is moored alongside the slipway.

Close by, a licensed pulling boat fitted with a basic sailing rig, was one of many similar craft which transported people including shipping agents to and from vessels at the Tail of the Bank anchorage.

Much of this scene vanished during 1892–1894 when the Glasgow & South Western Railway Company built another Princes Pier Station, a handsome Victorian building. It was knocked down in the late 1960s to make way for a container terminal which has recently become the multi-purpose Greenock Ocean Terminal.

Esplanade

Greenock Corporation built the Esplanade in the 1860s, using the spoil produced from constructing the Albert Harbour. The Old West Kirk, at the Campbell Street corner, had been originally erected in 1589–1591 on the waterfront site by the Westburn, now at the bottom of Nicolson Street. It was moved to this location during the 1920s. The church has stained glass windows by Sir Edward Burne-Jones, Dante Gabriel Rossetti and Daniel Cottier among its features, while the kirkyard contains many splendid old gravestones including a Greenock Gardeners' Society memorial tablet.

Along the road, Sandringham Terrace, a four-storey red sandstone block of tenements built in 1900–1901, is the finest property of its period in Greenock. Most attractive tiles illustrating the Firth of Clyde area decorate some closes. Seafield Cottage, nearby, is a Georgian house with an elegant ironwork porch where Robert Wallace of Kelly, Greenock's first MP – widely known for postal reform in the 1800s – lived at the end of his life. Adjoining Madeira Street, the Corinthian column and its attendant lamppost carry green navigation lights to guide shipping into the Tail of the Bank anchorage. Previously, the column stood much further eastwards, marking the Customs & Excise boundary on the river.

A Clyde Lighthouses Trust buoy, further west, is on public display opposite its original Roseneath Patch mooring. Dating from 1880, it was the first flashing light buoy to aid navigation on the river. On the other side of the road beside Roseneath Street, the John Galt Memorial Drinking Fountain, seen in this picture, commemorates the outstanding Scottish novelist and playwright who lived in Greenock from time to time.

Further on still, there is the red brick clubhouse of the Royal West of Scotland Amateur Boat Club, founded in 1866, whose members participate in rowing, dinghy sailing and canoeing.

Today, the Esplanade is regarded as one of the best promenades on Clydeside.

Seafield House

Seafield House was constructed during 1837 – the year Queen Victoria came to the throne – on a Brougham Street site overlooking Clyde Crescent and the waterfront. Later road development resulted in the mansion fronting the Esplanade, near Campbell Street. Its first owner was Robert Angus, a partner in the shipchandlery firm of Ewing May & Company who had premises in Bogle Street. His occupancy lasted forty years. The next resident was James Tennant Caird of Caird & Company, the important local shipbuilders noted for P&O passenger liners. A keen art-lover, he soon enlarged the building by adding a picture gallery to accommodate his collection of paintings.

When the Caird family moved elsewhere, Seafield House was sold to the Caledonian Railway Company. About 1867, the first tenancy was secured by William Orr, proprietor of a marine blockmaking business on Cross Shore Street. He

later owned, in partnership with other businessmen, a fleet of sailing ships which traded between Greenock and Quebec, loading coal outwards and timber on the homeward voyage. In due course, John Scott, Chairman of Scotts' Shipbuilding & Engineering Company Limited succeeded him in the house. He was a collector of rare Scottish books and used the art gallery block to hold a fine library.

Around 1907, the railway company sold the house to the Admiralty for use by the Royal Naval Volunteer Reserve, it serving as their Greenock headquarters for fourteen years. During 1921, Harland & Wolff Limited acquired Seafield House as the spacious grounds made an excellent new location for the Old West Kirk which obstructed the proposed development of the shipyards they had just taken over from Caird & Company. While the church was being repositioned, Seafield House contained living quarters for a number of their

Installing Electric Tramway Overhead Equipment

employees. After the company unfortunately closed the yard in 1927, the house was sporadically used by the Boy Scouts and various other youth groups. With the coming of the Second World War, the Air Training Corps took over the building. Thereafter, during 1950–1962, it was the turn of the Territorial Army to use the building. On moving out, they left a valuable extension in the form of a badminton hall. Seafield House was then taken over by the Corporation of Greenock who adapted it as a replacement for the Erskine Orr Hall in Crawford (Crawfurd) Street which was about to be knocked down. For most of the 1960s it was used by the Women's Royal Voluntary Service and several other organisations. After years of subsequent neglect, Seafield House was demolished in 1976 by Inverclyde District Council. Its place nowadays has been taken by a sheltered housing complex for elderly people.

From 1898, the Greenock & Port Glasgow Tramways Company set about introducing electric tram services to Greenock, Port Glasgow and Gourock in place of horse tram operations. Reconstruction of the existing track lines began at the end of 1900. This 1901 photograph shows workmen on Eldon Street, between Fox Street and Johnston Street, erecting one of the steel poles which carried the tramway powerlines above the middle of the road for travel in both directions.

Balclutha

Balclutha, one of the largest and finest mansions in Greenock with most extensive grounds, was built around 1857 on a prime spot in the West End facing Newark Street, ultimately also bordered by Madeira Street and Finnart Street. James Morton, founder of the Greenock Iron Company, ironmerchants, was its original owner. Provost of Greenock in 1868–1871, he encouraged the provision of better housing and good education in the town.

Everything about Balclutha was magnificent. The great hall and gallery formed a vast reception area used for high society banquets, business receptions and other grand occasions. Even the parkland gates – featuring Burmese teakwood with elaborate ironwork panels – were a striking characteristic of the property. James Morton's residency ended in the 1880s.

During 1888–1892, Balclutha was occupied by Sir Charles Cameron, the *North British Daily Mail* proprietor who became a Glasgow MP responsible for penal reforms, widening the franchise and changes to the liquor licensing laws in Scotland. J Milne Barbour was the subsequent owner for two or three years. Afterwards, Robert (later Sir Robert) McAlpine, founder of Sir Robert McAlpine & Sons Limited, the major public works contractor, took up ownership of the house. Balclutha Limited was a subsidiary company of his main business

(above, opposite) Balclutha

(below, opposite)
James Morton, Provost of Greenock, who first owned the house

(above)
this view of the dining room during the tenure of Robert L Scott, Chairman of Scotts' Shipbuilding and Engineering Company Ltd, features an elephant head hunting trophy and items from his collection of arms and armour

providing specialist plasterwork like ceiling mouldings for hotels, mansions and so on.

In turn, Robert L Scott, Chairman of Scotts' Shipbuilding & Engineering Company Limited, owned Balclutha from 1911 until his death in 1939. Much admired as a businessman, he was also an eminent collector of European arms and armour. This huge fascinating collection – including a knight on horseback which formed a really memorable spectacle in the hall of the mansion – is now in Glasgow's Kelvingrove Art Gallery & Museum. R L Scott had further status as a noted big-game hunter who led several expeditions, sometimes with a field naturalist in the party, to various parts of the world such as Africa, India, Europe and Canada. Many trophies and specimens from these adventures, of course, were displayed around the building as well – several, like a huge crocodile which used to frighten some of his visitors, now being on display in the McLean Museum.

On the outbreak of the Second World War, Balclutha was purchased by the Admiralty and used throughout the conflict for billeting members of the Women's Royal Naval Service. They must have found the building an impressive one despite the unfortunate circumstances. When peacetime was restored, the Admiralty converted Balclutha into a hostel for the staff of HM Torpedo Experimental Establishment at Fort Matilda, better known earlier as the Clyde Royal Naval Torpedo Factory. It served in this role for almost ten years. During 1956,

(left) the living room of Balclutha

(above) another dining room scene

Greenock Corporation became interested in taking over Balclutha for conversion into an old people's home but took no further action. Then, almost simultaneously, the mansion and its grounds were acquired by D McEwing & Sons Limited, a local building contractor, for development as a 48-residence housing estate.

So, Balclutha was duly knocked down in 1956–1957 – Chindwin, a villa on the Esplanade, acquiring its entrance gates and Cartsburn Augustine Church, now Cartsdyke Parish Church, being given the great chandelier which hung from the hall dome, some fine wood panelling and the beautiful main stairway oak balustrades for use as a rail round the choir range. The houses, though, were never built since Renfrewshire County Council, the local education authority, obtained the Balclutha site under a Compulsory Purchase Order for the construction of Greenock Academy's modern premises which opened some years later.

A Sugar Refiner's Rover Car

Walter G Neill of Neill Dempster & Neill, the local sugar refining
company, posed with his Rover 6 automobile for this photograph
during 1909 at Glenfield, his parent's house on Bedford Street, now a
nursing home. A two-seater body was the simplest version of the car.
They were first built in 1905 to a design by Edmund W Lewis
concentrating on quality and simplicity which produced good vehicles.
Competitive pricing allowed them to be among the least expensive
models on the market. Its single-cylinder 6 HP engine was mounted on
a wooden chassis reinforced with steel plates. According to an
intriguing report in *Autocar* magazine, the engine ignition switch
mounted on the dashboard "could, if necessary, be operated by the toe
of the driver's left boot".

Until factory-fitted windscreens and hoods to provide shelter became
available, owners sometimes installed an improvised form of protection
themselves. The neat canvas dodger on Walter Neill's vehicle must
have been specially made by a local sailmaker.

Popular around the country and overseas, these automobiles were in
production until 1911. Walter G Neill bought this Rover 6 in
Lochgilphead, his family owning Keills House and sporting estate near
Tayvallich, hence its Argyllshire SB 67 registration mark instead of
Greenock number plates.

Clyde Royal Naval Torpedo Factory

Admiralty contractors built the Clyde Royal Naval Torpedo Factory at Fort Matilda during 1907–1910. This view shows the plant just before its completion. It was constructed because the recent establishment of a new torpedo testing station in Loch Long – the increasing range of torpedoes had outgrown the capacity of the original Chatham testing station – necessitated a torpedo factory nearby. Around 700 workers were transferred from Woolwich Royal Arsenal, aggravating an already serious housing problem in the town which continued for many years. The buildings comprising a design unit, the main production hall, technical sections, a testing house, workshops, offices and ancillary premises were erected with stone from local quarries. Low rooflines ensured that the amenity of the district was not upset in any way. Secure accommodation was provided for storing the torpedoes and special arrangements were made for taking them to an adjacent jetty for shipment.

In the First World War, design and manufacture of

torpedoes proceeded simultaneously at the works. Security measures stopped trams picking up or dropping off passengers at the factory, meant people could not travel on their top decks until a bombproof screen was erected along the boundary railings and resulted in sentries checking all travellers and parcels on the tramcars. During peace, afterwards, work proceeded in the normal way. When the Second World War began, research projects were halted as every effort had to be directed into making torpedoes for war requirements – a canteen was even opened to ensure reasonable food for the workers. Some 3,000–4,000 people were employed in the factory at this point. Development of new torpedoes started again towards the end of the war. Later, however, the decision was taken to transfer production to a more suitable factory in Alexandria. Opening the Alexandria Royal Naval Torpedo Factory allowed the Greenock works to become HM Torpedo Experimental Establishment, concentrating on the research and design of new torpedoes until its closure in 1959.

Battery Park

Early in the 1900s, much land along the shore at Fort Matilda was still just common ground used by the community for various purposes. It was used by Drums Farm for animal grazing. Greenock Wanderers Rugby Football Club and other sports organisations held matches and the Volunteers – a forerunner of the Territorial Army – had parades and training camps. Paul Jones Son & Company also ran a boatbuilding business here. The site became known as the Battery Park from the presence of the fort with its 68-pounder guns.

During 1907, when the Admiralty compulsorily obtained some of the ground to erect the Clyde Royal Naval Torpedo Factory, many townspeople expressed concern about subsequent development bringing about the complete loss of a valuable public asset. Eventually, in a considerate response, Sir Hugh Shaw Stewart, the town's principal landowner, gifted the remaining open space to Greenock Corporation, so that a park could stay at this location.

In World War I and for a brief period after, the Scottish Concrete Shipbuilding Company occupied an area in the Battery Park to build concrete vessels. The firm was established because of the limited availability of steel for shipbuilding and the urgent need for cargo freighters at that time.

Just strolling along the broad park avenues and looking at the wonderful view – especially at sunset – was a most popular activity in the 1920s and the 1930s. During the Second World War, the Royal Air Force's Coastal Command had a flying boat base at the park waterfront. Thereafter, in peacetime, everybody was really able to enjoy themselves once again. On a single day in the summer of 1947 alone, 500 bathers took a dip in the open-air swimming pool. Since then, the Battery Park has welcomed circuses, dog shows, funfairs and firework displays It has even provided medical emergency helicopter landing pad facilities to ensure casualties reached Inverclyde Royal Hospital quickly. Sports facilities in the park have been upgraded in recent years.

Paul Jones Son & Company, Boatbuilders

Paul Jones Son & Company, yachtbuilders and boatbuilders, were in business throughout the halcyon days of yachting in the 1800s and early 1900s. The yard began at Quarry Quay in the Shore Street area of Gourock about 1870 but it was soon transferred to premises on early common land in Greenock leased from Sir Hugh Shaw Stewart, the town's laird, which became the Battery Park. Wood boat construction was carried out with repairs, maintenance and storage of wood, iron and steel vessels being undertaken as well.

An early vessel, *Virginia*, was a smart and able steam schooner, 29 tons, built in 1878 for W Nutter, an English yachtsman. During 1884, the Admiralty ordered seven sailing boats, 32 feet in length and capable of carrying at least twelve men, for the relief expedition attempting to free General Charles Gordon, Governor-General of the Sudan, who was besieged in Khartoum by rebel forces. Deck awnings were provided on these craft. In 1889, *Leprechaun*, a 3-ton cutter, was delivered to Henry C Falkner, Dublin fitted with sails from Joseph Pennell & Company of the Glebe Sailworks in the Albert Harbour. Around 1891, the slipway was reconstructed and new winch equipment installed allowing the handling of vessels up to 200 tons. Simultaneously, the West of Scotland Yacht Club in Greenock commissioned *Mallard*, *Teal* and *Widgeon*, a class of pleasure sailing boats, 19 feet long, simply equipped with a jib and lugsail, for use by their members. The 21-ton yacht tender, *Express*, also received an interior overhaul. *Wyniard*, 3 tons, a racing boat with a sail area of 390 square feet was built in 1893 to an acclaimed design by John Paterson & Harry M Paterson, a Greenock yacht design partnership. During 1895, the yard supplied a 5-ton teakwood motor launch powered by a Daimler petrol engine and fitted with top quality furnishings to the Rajah of Rahore in India. A similar craft was also built at this point for the Rajah of Baroda to use exploring India's rivers and inland waterways. So that elephants could haul it through the jungle, a 4-wheeled trolley was supplied with the vessel. A Thun, Rio de Janeiro, Brazil then took delivery of the Daimler motorboats *Ivona*, 41 feet long, capable of 8 knots and *Johanna*, 55 feet in length, a twin screw vessel. *Trilby*, a yawl of 12 tons, another commission at this time, was an impressive cruising yacht with a modern profile and a handy sail plan, only scrapped after long service in 1963. Moreover, a

(above)
Paul Jones Son & Company's boatyard
at the Battery Park photographed
shortly before its closure in 1927

(right)
Stradella, the biggest and smartest
steam yacht to be built by the yard

cutter of 11 tons, *Phantom*, was fitted-out for the sailing season and a 12-ton lugger, *Helena*, owned by P M Coats of Paisley, was crated for shipment to the Nice Regattas.

During 1896, Alexander Jones became the junior partner in the firm. Further land was obtained for the boatyard. Over the year, more than 20 vessels were constructed including *Myrtle* for John Neill of Neill Dempster & Neill, sugar refiners in Drumfrochar Road; a steam yacht of 60 tons; motor launches like *Wacketera*, the first of a series designed by Alexander Jones; centreboard sloops for Irish owners and *Xantho*, one of a class of small racing yachts for Innellan Corinthian Yacht Club members. *Salmon*, a little centreboard yacht, was redecked as well. Meanwhile, 4 motor workboats on show at the Imperial Institute Yachting Exhibition in London encouraged more orders. In 1897, the first of a new class of yacht was built for sailing on the Nile. A spacious launch fitted with a crane was supplied later for deerstalking service on Loch Morar. Some dainty punts attracted favourable comment. *Snarleyow* and *Noyra*, 21 tons and 43 feet long, built in 1899 for A F Maclaren, Skelmorlie and Matthew Greenlees, Paisley were powerful racing cutters in a class of yachts crewed by 7–9 persons. At the same time, extra ground was secured for the yard and a new building shed was erected to improve the facilities. Prospective sale preparations were also carried out on *Claymore*, a steel 36-ton screw cutter, prior to the vessel being sold to the French government for service in naval dockyards.

Stradella was a schooner-rigged steam yacht built in 1901 over a period of eight months for David N Bertram, Acting Director, Bertram's Limited, engineers and millwrights, Edinburgh, to a design by G L Watson & Company, the eminent naval architects in Glasgow. This splendid 69-ton vessel, 81 feet in length 14 feet in beam and 6 feet in hull depth to the waterline, provided with a spacious promenade deck and fitted with electric light, was the largest ship constructed by the yard. A crew of five comprised the master, engineer, cook, a deckhand-steward and a deckhand-stoker. Shelter on deck was available in the deckhouse saloon. The owner's accommodation constituted a saloon comfortably furnished with two large couches, a fine table, cabinets and buffets; the stateroom containing two beds, a wardrobe and washhand basin and a bathroom which had a folding washbasin, full-size teak bath and a lavatory. Each of two passenger staterooms featured a small couch, two bunks, a neat wardrobe and a washbasin. A lavatory was situated between them. The crew's quarters had seating with a table, locker space, an enormous bread bin, five cots and a bucket WC. A dinghy and liferaft facilities exceeded safety requirements. Galley equipment included a coal-fired range together with a meat safe on deck in the stern. The pantry had a sink, dresser and storage facilities. An economic 11 HP Bertram's engine with a single propeller gave a top speed of 9 knots and the large coal bunker capacity provided an excellent steaming range of about 2,000 miles.

Stradella was sold to several other British yachtsmen in later years. William L Macfie, Macfie & Sons, sugar refiners, Liverpool, who owned the vessel during the 1920s and 1930s was a member of the remarkable Greenock family who had been promoters of the sugar refining industry, civic affairs and philanthropy in the town during the 1800s. In service, the ship usually cruised to places around Great Britain, particularly in the Highlands and Islands of Scotland, with some voyages to destinations elsewhere in Europe. Latterly, however, this steam yacht just served as a houseboat. *Stradella* was broken up in 1953.

In 1902, the iron 56-ton steam yacht *Maritana* arrived at the yard for hull plate damage repairs after going aground at Wemyss Bay. *Lobelia*, a screw schooner of 130 tons, became the largest vessel to use its services. A sturdy motor launch, *Kinloch*, 18 tons and 43 feet long, equipped with auxiliary sails, was commissioned by Sir George Bullough, Rum during 1903 to provide transport between the island and the Scottish mainland. *Kinloch* was sold to other owners and scrapped by 1911.

Over the winter of 1903–1904, the boatyard resembled a yachting exhibition as there was around sixty craft totalling 2,050 tons in its storage area. Among these vessels, *Snowflake*, a steam ketch of 48 tons, was owned by Charles R Kincaid and John G Kincaid of John G Kincaid & Company, marine engineers, Greenock. High quality yacht boats, including a launch, were built in 1904 for *Grianaig*, the new steam yacht being constructed for Robert Sinclair Scott by Scotts' Shipbuilding & Engineering Company Limited. *Iris*, a 68-ton screw sloop, attended the yard for a survey and the yawl, *Mafalda*, 17 tons, required hull recoppering. Later, newly built gigs secured approval from the owners for the standard of craftsmanship. Some motorboats were also beautifully made in cedarwood. T Steventon, Glasgow commissioned *Olive* in 1908, another of the series of motor launches designed by Alexander Jones. A local businessman, R MacKean Agnew, became the sole proprietor of the yard about 1910, but continued the firm under its original name. During 1915, *Roy*, 35 or so feet long, a harbour launch suitable for one-man operation, was built for the Clyde Marine Motoring Company at Princes Pier and carried pilots to and from ships in the Gareloch during the First World War. Some years later, a 7-ton cabin cruiser, ten lifeboats and dinghies were supplied to various customers. *Frolic*, a tiny open centreboard yacht commissioned in 1924 by James A Ewing, a Lancashire yachtsman, was one of the last boats built by the yard.

A well-known and respected business, Paul Jones Son & Company produced almost 150 vessels. Some yachtsmen had several boats built by the yard. Closure took place in 1927 when its ground lease expired and could not be extended because the Corporation of Greenock had accepted the gift of the Battery Park from Sir Hugh Shaw Stewart on terms which prevented the firm remaining at the site.

Dunrod Quarries

Peter Cram, John Coghill & Company and Robert W Jamieson of A & R Jamieson, building contractors in Greenock, opened the three Dunrod Quarries in Shielhill Glen about 1860. Much of their excellent grey sandstone provided the material for house building in central areas of the town. The main photograph shows one quarry with typical stone crushing equipment for the production of aggregate in miscellaneous grades, transport facilities and a blacksmith's wooden shanty workshop containing a gas furnace supplied with energy from the outdoor tank.

At first, the stone was taken away by horse and cart along a farm access track, specially paved with hewn slabs of stone in an effort to make a proper thoroughfare, then into the town on the old main road from Inverkip. But from 1868, Caledonian Railway Company trains using 7-ton freight wagons conveyed it out of the valley to Greenock on a branch line – which included a tunnel and sidings – specially constructed along the southern bank of the Kip Water past Majeston Farm to the Glasgow–Wemyss Bay railway below Dunrod Hill and then into Upper Greenock Station Depot.

Bernard 'Barney' McGechan and Neil McGilp, Irish labourers, carried on the maintenance of the railway line from a works hut known as Barney's Box. They were also responsible for ensuring that country traffic was not endangered when a train was proceeding over the roads at level crossings. One by one, during 1876–1885, the Dunrod Quarries closed as their material ran out. Total production came to over 250,000 tons of sandstone.

Nowadays, Peter Cram's quarry is still visible from Clyde Muirshiel Regional Park's Shielhill Nature Trail and vestiges of the other quarries remain among the adjacent woodland.

Dunrod quarries provided much of the stone for buildings in Greenock until their closure in 1885. The two lower photographs are present day views of the quarry road and the winding route of the railway

A Charabanc Tour

Early in the 1900s, only the more affluent people in a community could afford to own a car so many folk relied on charabancs to provide a means of visiting the coast or country. Public services were available to various destinations around Greenock and local organisations such as church groups, the Salvation Army, and trade associations frequently arranged private charabanc trips to various places on Clydeside.

Here is a crowd of Greenock grocers and their families in well-filled charabancs on a private Three Lochs day tour during the 1920s, seen at Arrochar Hotel during a refreshment stop. On leaving town, this outing had crossed the Clyde on the Erskine Ferry and driven past Loch Lomond to Arrochar. From there, it continued down Loch Long then along the Gareloch back to the Erskine Ferry for the last stretch homewards.

All the charabancs belonged to P & J Beaton, transport contractors, Greenock. The lead vehicle, driven by James Beaton, VS 259, was an Albion; the middle charabanc was a Thornycroft with William Calder as the driver; and the last vehicle, VS 1029, was another Albion driven by Joe King. Each of the petrol engined, chain-driven charabancs with a top speed of about 15 miles an hour had carbide lamps, wooden mudguards, solid tyres and bodies which were interchangeable with lorry bodies.

Naturally, these charabanc excursions were very popular events. Colourful streamers sometimes emphasised their atmosphere of joyful relaxation. Many people in Greenock found them memorable activities because they provided a welcome respite from ordinary life, surrounded by the great drab establishments of commerce and industry located in the town.

Thomas Kincaid, a local character

Thomas Kincaid, a peddler, joined the community from Ireland at the age of 45 in 1890. He quickly became known to everybody as 'Tommy Matches' since matchsticks formed the principal commodity among his wares.

He was a simple fellow whose disconsolate features harmonised perfectly with his shabby clothes. Any dignity perhaps imparted to his appearance by a full beard was dissipated by a shambling gait and watery eyes, nose and mouth. Although quiet and inoffensive, Tommy did not escape the cheeky attentions of street urchins who sometimes pulled his coat and yelled after him "Tommy Matches; Tommy Matches" in deliberate bids to provoke an irate response for their own amusement. Working men also had rough fun with Tommy by fixing an unwanted appeal for charity to his cap and so on. However, he never retaliated in any way and his tormentors found little reward in teasing such a dull victim for very long.

Tommy's pitches were scattered around the town, a favourite one being in Bank Street. His stock of matchsticks along with ancillary items like buttons, shoelaces and ribbons was exhibited in a wooden sales box prominently labelled 'Matches' given to him by a kindly shopkeeper. One customer was moved to quip, "I suppose we'll need to call you a timber merchant!" in a thoughtless moment. "No, you'll not, I'm a general merchant" was the brave answer. A corner of Tommy's display box was also used as a cash till. Of course, he was quite unable to administer money, trusting customers to pay the proper amount. So, inevitably, a few scoundrels paid with counterfeit coins and foreign currency or took more change than was necessary.

There was amusement and despair when Tommy varied his profession and appeared as a street musician with a wheezy old concertina. Naturally, he had no musical knowledge and just pressed its keys haphazardly while he manipulated the bellows. A dreadful cacophony was the unavoidable result. Whenever Tommy was requested by someone to play a particular melody, he would gravely nod his head in a sign of comprehension but just keep on performing in the same

hopeless way. Mourners attending a church funeral service were sometimes irritated by Tommy's coincidental playing at a nearby location, the solemn nature of the proceedings being rather lost. Nobody ever succeeded in persuading him to respect these occasions. Tommy also often disturbed the serenity of the Regent Street neighbourhood with his atrocious musical entertainment. Eventually, residents took collective action for his own good and theirs by giving him a small barrel organ whose notes were a preferable substitute for the appalling noise of his concertina.

When Thomas Kincaid was about 53, illness brought him to the notice of the local authorities and from then on he became, at times, an inmate of Smithston Poorhouse & Asylum, later Ravenscraig Hospital. He died there in 1910.

References

AULD, W *Greenock and its Early Social Environment*, 1907

BOLTON, J S *The Old West Kirk 1591–1991*, 1991

BROWN, A *The Early Annals of Greenock*, 1924

CAMPBELL, D *Historical Sketches of Greenock*, 2 volumes, 1879 and 1881

CORMACK I L *Tramways of Greenock, Gourock and Port Glasgow*, 1975

DONALD, J *Old Greenock Characters*, 2 volumes 1920 and 1930

DOW, J L *Greenock*, 1975

GREENOCK CORPORATION *Gas Undertaking Centenary 1828–1928*, 1928

HAMILTON, J T *The Mid Kirk of Greenock*, 1991

HAMILTON, T W *How Greenock Grew*, 1947

MACDOUGALL, S *Profiles from the Past*, 1982

METHVEN, C W *Sketches of Greenock and its Harbours in 1886*, 1886

SMITH, R M *The History of Greenock*, 1921

SNODDY, T G *Round about Greenock*, 1937

WEIR, D *History of the Town of Greenock*, 1829

WILLIAMSON, A *Views and Reminiscences of Old Greenock*, 1891

WILLIAMSON, G *Old Cartsburn*, 1894

WILLIAMSON, G *Old Greenock*, 2 volumes, 1886 and 1888